Car Sales Confidence for New Salespeople

How to Build Confidence, Handle Rejection, and Succeed on the Sales Floor

Bruce Huddleston

Bedrock Heritage Publishing

DISCLAIMER

This book is based on the author's personal and professional experiences, observations, and opinions, accumulated over a 35-year career in the automotive industry. It is intended for educational and informational purposes only.

The stories and anecdotes contained in this book are drawn from real-world situations encountered throughout the author's career. However, names, identifying details, specific circumstances, employer names, dealership names, and individual characteristics have been changed, omitted, combined, or fictionalized to protect the privacy of the individuals involved. Any resemblance to specific living persons, current or former employers, or existing businesses is coincidental and unintentional.

No individual, dealership, organization, or employer referenced or implied in the stories within this book has reviewed, approved, or endorsed the content herein. The recollections and characterizations presented are solely the author's own perspective and memory of events and do not constitute a factual record, legal testimony, or statement of fact regarding any identifiable person or entity.

The sales strategies, techniques, and professional advice presented in this book reflect the author's personal approach and experience. Individual results will vary based on experience, effort, market conditions, dealership policies, and other factors beyond the author's control. Nothing in this book constitutes a guarantee of income, employment, or professional outcome.

The author and publisher have made reasonable efforts to ensure the accuracy of information presented at the time of writing. The author and publisher make no representations or warranties regarding the completeness, accuracy, or current applicability of the information contained herein, and expressly disclaim any liability arising from the use or application of the content of this book.

By reading this book, you acknowledge and agree that the author and publisher shall not be liable for any damages, losses, or claims arising directly or indirectly from the use of or reliance upon any information contained herein.

A Free Bonus For Readers

Your Complete Digital Script Library

Get the Car Sales Survival Quick-Reference Card — a free companion to this book that puts the key rules and techniques on one page you can keep at your desk.

Visit:

www.carsalessurvivalseries.com/scripts

Enter your email to claim your free reader bonus.

Print it. Keep it. Use it.

CONTENTS

Introduction

Confidence Is a Skill, Not a Personality

Let me get one thing out of the way before we start.

You are not missing some gene that confident people have. There is no confidence gene. The salesperson on your floor who walks up to strangers all day like it's nothing wasn't born that way. I promise you he wasn't. Somewhere back there, he was standing exactly where you're standing now, watching a customer pull in, feeling his stomach drop.

He just did it enough times that it stopped dropping.

That's the whole secret, and I'm going to spend this book unpacking it. Confidence is not a personality type. It's not something you either have or don't. It is a skill. It is built. And anything that can be built can be built by you.

I spent thirty-five years in this business. I started as a kid who needed a job and ended up running departments and training hundreds of salespeople. In all that time, I never once met a natural. I met people who'd already done the reps. That's it. The ones who looked fearless had just been scared earlier, in private, where you couldn't see it.

Here's why this matters more than almost anything else I could teach you.

Most new salespeople don't wash out because they don't know what to say. You can learn what to say in an afternoon. They wash out because they can't make themselves walk across the lot and say it. They see the customer. They hesitate. They wait for someone else to take the up. Or they walk out there so tentatively that the customer reads the fear before they hear the hello.

Fear costs new salespeople more deals than any skill gap ever will. I've watched it happen for three decades. It is the number one thing standing between a new person and a paycheck. Not product knowledge. Not a closing technique. Fear.

So that's what this book is about. Not what to say—the other books in this series cover that. This one is about what happens inside you before a single word comes out. The freeze. The hesitation. The voice in your head that says wait, not yet, let somebody else get this one.

I'm going to be straight with you the whole way through, because you deserve that and because pretending the fear isn't real would insult you. The fear is real. It's normal. Everybody had it. And I am not going to tell you to believe in yourself, or that you've got this, or any of that empty stuff that feels good for about four seconds and changes nothing.

I'm going to give you something better. I'm going to show you what confidence actually is, where it actually comes from, and exactly what to do to build it. Preparation. Reps. A healthier relationship with the word no. Concrete things you can do to start your next shift.

Because confidence you can feel but can't act on is worthless, the goal isn't to feel brave. The goal is to walk across that lot. Everything in this book points back to something you can do, not something you're supposed to magically feel.

Confidence is a skill. Let's go build it.

The Rule: Confidence is not something you're born with. It's something you build—so start building.

Chapter 1

Why New Salespeople Freeze

L ET ME DESCRIBE THE moment, because you know it even if nobody's ever named it for you.

A car pulls onto the lot. You see it through the glass. And something in your body locks up. Your feet get heavy. You find a reason — any reason — to look busy for just a few more seconds. Maybe you can straighten some brochures. Maybe you suddenly need to check something on the computer. Maybe you just stand there and watch, hoping someone else will move first.

That's the freeze. And if it's happening to you, I want you to hear this clearly: there is nothing wrong with you. The freeze is the single most universal experience among new salespeople. Every veteran on your floor did it. I did it.

But let me also be straight about what it costs, because nobody wins by pretending it's harmless.

While you're frozen, one of two things happens. Either somebody else takes your customer — and your paycheck — or you eventually go out there, late, stiff, and apologetic, and the customer feels every bit of it.

Here's the part most new people don't understand. The customer cannot read your mind. They don't know you're scared. They can't tell the difference between a salesperson who's terrified and a salesperson who doesn't care.

From their side of the lot, both look the same: like nobody wants to help them.

So your fear, which feels so private and so loud inside your head, shows up to the customer as coldness. As indifference. You think you're hiding it. You're not hiding it—you're broadcasting something worse.

FROM THE FLOOR

The summer heat in Texas is no joke. I was managing a used-car lot — no air conditioning on the lot, obviously — and it was one of those July afternoons when the asphalt is soft, and the air feels like a wet towel. A couple pulled in. I watched my newest salesperson sprint out to meet them — which was already the wrong move — and by the time he got to them, he was visibly sweating through his shirt. The customers looked at him, looked at each other, and said they were just looking. He came back inside looking defeated.

I went out. Introduced myself. Said: "Sorry about the heat — let me know if you want to step inside and cool off while we talk." That's all it took. They came inside. We sold them a car in ninety minutes. The first salesperson did everything wrong before he said a word. I did one thing right: I acknowledged where they were before I asked anything of them.

Look at what actually happened there.

The new kid wasn't lazy. He wasn't uncaring. If anything, he cared too much — that's why he sprinted, that's why he sweated, that's why he came back inside crushed. His fear made him overcorrect into a frantic mess, and the customers read it instantly. Then I walked out at a normal pace, said one human thing, and they relaxed.

The difference between us wasn't courage and cowardice. It was reps. I'd made that walk ten thousand times. He'd made it a dozen. That's the entire gap.

So why does the freeze happen? Strip it down, and it's almost always one of three things.

You're afraid of being rejected.

The customer might brush you off, and somewhere in your head, a brush-off feels like a referendum on you as a person. We're going to dismantle that one completely in Chapter 3.

You're afraid of not knowing the answer.

You picture the customer asking something you can't answer, and you standing there exposed as a fraud. Chapter 7 takes that fear apart, too.

You haven't done it enough times yet.

This is the big one, and it's also the most fixable, because there's only one fix and it's the most reliable thing in this entire book: reps. The freeze melts with volume. Not with a pep talk. With volume.

Here's what I need you to take out of this chapter. The freeze is normal, it's temporary, and it is costing you right now — today — in deals you're not even aware you're losing. Naming it is the first step to beating it. You can't fix a thing you won't admit is happening.

You're going to feel the freeze again on your next shift. Good. Now you know what it is.

The Rule: The customer can't tell the difference between your fear and your lack of caring. From across the lot, both look like nobody came to help.

Chapter 2

What Confidence Actually Is (and What It Isn't)

Before we build confidence, we have to be clear about what it is. Because many new salespeople are chasing the wrong thing, and chasing the wrong thing will make you worse, not better.

Here's the confusion. New people watch the loudest guy on the floor — the back-slapper, the fast-talker, the one who never shuts up and never backs down — and they think that's confidence. So they try to become that. They turn up the volume. They get pushy. They talk over the customer. They figure if they just act bigger and harder, they'll look confident.

That's not confidence. That's the costume insecurity wears.

Real confidence and that loud act look nothing alike once you know what to watch for. Let me draw the line clean, because if you cross it, you'll spend years building the wrong thing.

Confidence is quiet. Bravado is loud.

The genuinely confident salesperson doesn't need to fill every silence or win every exchange. He's comfortable letting the customer talk. The insecure one can't stand a pause — every quiet moment feels like losing, so he keeps talking. Customers feel the difference in about ten seconds.

Confidence listens. Bravado performs.

A confident salesperson asks a question and actually waits for the answer. The loud guy asks a question and is already loading his next line while you're still talking. One of those makes you feel like a person. The other makes you feel like a target.

Confidence is secure. Bravado is desperate.

This is the heart of it. Real confidence comes from being settled — you know what you're doing, and you're okay with who you are, so you don't need anything from this particular customer to feel fine about yourself. Bravado needs the win. It's hungry, and customers smell the hunger, and the hunger is what makes them put their guard up.

Here's the test. Aggression, pushiness, the hard sell — every one of those comes from need. From "I have to have this deal." That need is not a strength. It's fear with its chest puffed out.

So what is real confidence, in plain terms?

It's certainty about what you're doing and security in who you are. That's it. Certainty comes from competence — you've prepared, you know your inventory, you know the process, so you're not afraid of getting caught out. Security comes from not hanging your whole self-worth on whether one stranger buys a car today.

Notice something about both of those. Neither one is loud. Neither one requires you to become someone customers can't stand.

This matters enormously for a nervous new person, because it means the path forward is not "get louder and harder." Thank God. If you're a quiet person reading this and thinking you'll have to turn into some obnoxious caricature to make it in this business, you don't. You'd actually be building the wrong thing.

The customer in front of you doesn't want a performance. They're about to spend a lot of money, and they're nervous too. What calms them down is a calm salesperson. Steady. Unhurried. Someone who clearly knows the drill and isn't going to pounce.

You don't get there by faking bigness. You get there by becoming competent and settling in. The rest of this book is how.

The Rule: Real confidence is quiet. If you have to perform it, it isn't confidence—it's insecurity in a louder shirt.

CHAPTER 3

THE FEAR OF REJECTION

IF I HAD TO point to the single root of most floor fear, it's this one. Almost everything we've talked about so far traces back here. The freeze, the hesitation, the loud overcompensating — underneath it all is usually the same thing. You're afraid the customer will reject you.

And in this business, they will. Constantly. "Just looking." "We're not buying today." The walk-off. The one who won't make eye contact. You are going to get told "No" more times in a month than most people get told "No" in a year.

So if "No" destroys you, you're in the wrong line of work — unless you change your relationship to the word. And you can. That's what this chapter is for.

Here's the trap new people fall into. A customer says, "Just looking," and you hear, "I don't like you." You're bad at this. You said something wrong. You carry it to the next customer, and now you're tentative with them, and they can feel it, and they brush you off too, and now you've got a spiral going. One "No" becomes a bad afternoon becomes a bad week.

The whole thing rests on a single false belief: that the "No" is about you. Most of the time, it isn't. It's rarely about you.

FROM THE FLOOR

I had a colleague who couldn't get any traction with a woman at the used-car lot. She kept saying she was just looking. He couldn't figure out what was off—he'd done everything right as far as he could tell. He came and got me.

I went out, introduced myself, and asked how I could help her.

She said: "God, thank you. I really want to buy this car. But that other guy looks exactly like my ex-husband, and I cannot stand the sight of him."

Nothing to do with the car. Nothing to do with the approach. She knew exactly what she wanted — she just needed a different person in front of her before she would let the conversation happen. We tested the vehicle, worked out fair numbers, and she drove home happy.

Don't take "I'm just looking" personally. Don't take it as a verdict. Take it as information — something needs to be adjusted. Sometimes that's your approach. Sometimes it's giving more space. And occasionally it's a different person entirely. All of those are workable. None of them is the end of the deal.

I tell that story to every nervous new salesperson I can, because it's the cleanest example I've ever seen of a truth you need bolted into your head. The "No" usually has nothing to do with you.

That woman's "just looking" had a reason, and the reason was a guy's face. My colleague did everything right. It didn't matter. And here's the thing—he took it personally. He came and got me because he thought he was failing. He wasn't failing. He just happened to look like somebody's ex-husband, which is not in any sales training manual ever written.

You will never know most of the reasons. The customer who brushes you off just got bad news from the doctor. They are embarrassed about their credit. Already bought it somewhere else and feel weird about it. Is just not a talker. The list is endless, and you are not on it.

So here's the reframe, and I want you to actually use it, not just nod at it.

A "No" is not a verdict. It's information.

A verdict is final, and it's about you. Information is neutral, and it's about the situation. When a customer says no, the confident salesperson doesn't think "I failed." He thinks, "Okay — something needs to adjust." Maybe the approach. Maybe give them more room. Maybe, like in that story, it just needs to be a different person. All workable problems. None of them is a judgment on your worth.

What this does to your fear.

Watch what happens when you stop taking "No" personally. The fear of asking drains right out. Because what were you actually afraid of? You were afraid of the "No" landing like a slap. Take away the slap — make it just information —, and there's nothing left to be afraid of. You can ask, hear no, shrug, and move to the next one without a scratch.

The salesperson who can take a "No" cleanly is the salesperson who stops being afraid to approach. Those are the same skills. Beat the fear of rejection, and you've beaten most of the freeze along with it.

You're going to hear "No" today. It's not about you. Go get the next one.

The Rule: A "No" is information, not a verdict. And most of the time, it isn't even about you.

CHAPTER 4

PREPARATION BEATS NERVES

EVERYTHING UP TO NOW has been about understanding the fear. Now we start killing it, and we start with the most reliable weapon you've got. It's not courage. Courage is unreliable — some days you feel it, most days you don't. The weapon is preparation.

Here's the principle, and it runs through the whole rest of this book: confidence is mostly just competence you can feel.

Think about why you're nervous walking up to a customer. Strip it down, and most of the fear is fear of the unknown. What if they ask something I can't answer? What if I blank on the price? What if they want to see the truck and I don't know where the keys are? What if I freeze?

Every one of those is a what-if. And here's the beautiful thing about a what-if: you can shut it down ahead of time. You can't talk yourself out of fear in the moment — try it, it doesn't work. But you can prepare your way out of it before the moment ever arrives.

The prepared salesperson has far less to be afraid of, because far less can catch him off guard. That's not a mindset trick. That's just true. Let me show you what to actually prepare.

Know your inventory.

Not every spec on every unit — nobody has that on day one. But know what's on your lot. Know your three or four most popular units cold: the features, the rough price, who they're right for. Walk the lot before your shift. Sit in the vehicles. Open the hoods. When a customer points at something, you want to already know it, not be discovering it alongside them.

Have your openers ready.

The freeze is worst when you don't know what's going to come out of your mouth. So decide in advance. Have two or three opening lines you're comfortable with, ready to go, so the first words aren't a gamble. We're not scripting a whole conversation — just removing the terror of the first sentence. When you already know how you're going to open, the walk across the lot gets a lot shorter.

Know the process.

Know the steps of a deal at your store. Greeting, needs, vehicle, demo drive, numbers — whatever your store's flow is, know it so you always know what comes next. A huge amount of new-person panic is just not knowing what you're supposed to do next. Take that away, and you walk around a lot calmer.

Prepare your body and your day.

Show up early. Dress like a professional. Get your keys, your tools, and your head straight before the first car pulls in. Walking onto the floor already behind and scrambling are guaranteed ways to feel rattled all day. Walking on prepared and early is how you feel ready.

Now here's what I love about preparation as the cure for fear: it's the part you have total control over. You can't control whether the customer's nice. You can't control traffic, or your credit-challenged ups, or whether somebody walks. But you can absolutely control whether you walked your lot this morning and know your units. That's all yours.

And it compounds. The prepared salesperson has a good interaction, which builds a little confidence, which makes him prepare more, which makes the next one better. Preparation doesn't just lower today's fear. It starts the whole flywheel turning.

You will never make the fear disappear by wishing. You make it shrink by being ready. The salesperson who knows his stuff has simply run out of things to be afraid of.

So before your next shift: walk the lot. Know your units. Have your opener. Then go to work like a person who's ready — because you will be.

The Rule: You can't talk yourself out of fear. But you can prepare your way out of it.

CHAPTER 5

THE FIRST APPROACH OF THE DAY

THERE'S A SPECIFIC KIND of fear that has nothing to do with how long you've been doing this. Even guys who've sold for years feel it. It's the first up of the day.

The first approach is the hardest one you'll make all shift. Not because it's harder in any real sense — the customer isn't tougher, the car isn't different — but because you're cold. You haven't warmed up. You've spent the morning building it up in your head, and now the first car pulls in and every bit of dread you've been marinating in since you woke up lands at once.

I want to talk about that first up specifically, because if you can crack it, the rest of the day mostly takes care of itself.

Why the first one is the worst?

Here's what's going on. The fear isn't really about the customer in front of you. It's about the buildup. You got to work, you saw a slow lot, and your brain started running scenarios. What if I blank? What if they're rude? What if I lose it in front of everybody? By the time a real customer shows up, you've already lost the fight three times in your imagination.

And the longer you wait, the worse it gets. Dread compounds. Every minute you stand there not going out makes the going out feel bigger. The salesperson who waits around for the right customer to warm up on is really just feeding the fear.

Go first. Go early. Go before you're ready.

The cure is almost stupidly simple. Take the first up fast, before the dread has time to build. Don't wait for the perfect customer. Don't wait until you feel ready — you won't feel ready, that's the whole problem. The feeling of readiness comes after you go, not before.

Some of the best salespeople I've managed had a private rule: I take the first car that pulls in, no matter what. Doesn't matter if it's raining, doesn't matter if I'm tired, doesn't matter if it looks like a tough one. First car's mine. They did it on purpose, to beat the buildup. Once that first one's behind you — even if it goes badly — the spell is broken. You've already done the scary thing. Everything after is just more reps.

Lower the stakes on the first one.

Part of what makes the first up terrifying is that you've turned it into a referendum. This is going to set the tone for my whole day. No, it isn't. It's one conversation with one person. Take the pressure off. The goal of the first approach isn't to sell a car — it's just to get moving. To break the ice on yourself. If you walk out there only trying to say hello and be useful, there's almost nothing left to fail at.

Build a pre-shift routine.

Veterans don't rely on willpower for this. They have a routine that carries them out the door. Walk the lot, check the units, settle the head, maybe one specific thing they always do before the floor opens. Whatever it is, it should end with you outside, moving, instead of inside, thinking. A routine beats motivation every time, because motivation is a feeling, and a routine is just what you do.

Here's the truth about the first up. It's a tax. You pay it once a day, every day, and then you're free to work. The salespeople who struggle are the ones trying to avoid paying it. The ones who do well just pay it early and get on with the shift.

Don't wait to feel brave. Take the first one. The brave feeling shows up afterward, every time.

The Rule: The first up is the hardest one you'll make all day. So make it fast — before the dread has time to grow.

CHAPTER 6

FAKING IT VS. BUILDING IT

YOU'VE HEARD "FAKE IT till you make it" your whole life. Somebody probably said it to you your first week on the floor. It's half good advice and half a trap, and nobody ever tells you which half is which. Let me sort it out, because getting this wrong will cost you, customers.

There are two completely different things people mean by "fake it," and they could not be more different in how they play out.

The good kind: borrowing the posture of confidence.

The first kind is acting calm when you don't feel calm. Standing tall when your stomach's in knots. Keeping your voice steady when your heart's pounding. Walking at a normal pace when everything in you wants to either bolt or freeze.

That kind of faking it is not only fine — it's one of the most useful tools you've got. Here's why it works. The customer can't see your insides. They can only see your outsides. If your outsides are calm, the customer relaxes, the interaction goes better, and a better interaction actually does make you more confident. You faked the posture, the posture got you a decent result, and the decent result was real. That's borrowed confidence, and it's a real bridge to the earned kind.

There's even something physical to it. Stand up straight, slow your breathing, plant your feet — and your nervous system starts to believe you a little. The calm body talks the nervous mind down. We'll get deeper into that in the next chapter. For now, just know this: acting the part of a calm professional is allowed, it's smart, and it works.

The dangerous kind: faking what you know.

Then there's the other kind of faking it, and this one will wreck you. This is faking knowledge you don't have. Bluffing. Making up an answer because you're scared that saying "I don't know" will expose you.

This blows up the second you're caught — and you will get caught. A customer asks if the truck has a tow package. You don't know, but you're scared to look unsure, so you say, "Yeah, sure it does." Then it doesn't. Now you're not the new guy who didn't know one spec. Now you're a liar. And the customer doesn't just distrust that one answer — they distrust everything you said before it and everything you'll say after. You torched the whole relationship to protect your ego for ten seconds.

Customers will forgive you for being new. They will not forgive you for lying to them. The first is a condition. The second is a choice.

The line, stated plainly.

So here's the line, and I want you to keep it sharp in your head.

Fake the posture. Never fake the facts.

Act calm when you're not — yes. Act certain about things you're not certain about — no. The moment "fake it till you make it" tips over from how you carry yourself into what you claim is true, it stops being confidence and starts being a con. And customers can smell a con.

The next chapter is going to show you that "I don't know, let me find out" isn't the weakness you think it is — it's actually one of the most confident things you can say. But it only works if you've kept your credibility intact. So protect it. Fake the calm all you want. Tell the truth about everything else.

The Rule: Fake the posture, never the facts. Acting calm builds confidence; bluffing a customer destroys trust the second you're caught.

CHAPTER 7

CONFIDENCE WHEN YOU DON'T HAVE THE ANSWER

ASK A NEW SALESPERSON what they're most afraid of on the floor, and a lot of them will tell you the same thing: the question they can't answer. They lie awake on it. The customer's going to ask something — about financing, about the engine, about some feature — and I'm going to stand there with nothing, and they're going to know I'm a fraud.

I want to take this fear apart completely, because it's built on a belief that's flat wrong.

The belief is: not knowing the answer exposes me as incompetent. The truth is: not knowing the answer is normal, expected, and completely survivable. What exposes you isn't the gap in your knowledge. It's how you handle the gap.

Nobody knows everything. Not even the veterans.

First, let's kill the fantasy that experienced salespeople have every answer. They don't. The business is too big. Too many models, too many trims, too many financing wrinkles, too many one-off questions. The thirty-year veteran gets asked things he doesn't know every single week. The difference is he's completely comfortable not knowing, because he learned a long time ago that not knowing isn't the problem.

You're holding yourself to a standard that the best people in the building don't even meet. Drop it.

The most confident sentence you're not using.

Here is one of the most powerful, confident things a salesperson can say:

"That's a great question. I don't know off the top of my head — let me find out for you."

Read that again, because new people hear it as an admission of weakness, and it is the opposite. Watch what it actually communicates. It says: I'm secure enough not to pretend. I respect you enough to get it right instead of guessing. I'd rather give you the truth than protect my ego. That is exactly what a confident professional sounds like.

Compare it to the alternative. A confident-sounding wrong answer feels good for a second and then detonates when the customer finds out — and customers do find out. A smooth, wrong "yes" is worse than an honest "let me check," every time, because one builds trust and the other destroys it.

How to handle the gap with composure.

The trick isn't knowing everything. It's staying composed when you don't. Here's the move. Don't flinch. Don't apologize all over yourself. Don't get that panicked look. Just acknowledge the question, say you'll get the answer, and then actually go get it. "Good question — give me two minutes, I'll find out exactly." Then come back with the real answer.

You've now done something most salespeople don't. You told the truth, and you followed through. The customer trusts you more than they did before they asked.

Notice that the composure is the whole thing. The same words — "I don't know" — land completely differently depending on whether you say them like you're ashamed or like it's no big deal. Say it like it's no big deal. Because it isn't.

The reframe.

So flip it in your head. The question you can't answer isn't a threat. It's an opportunity to show exactly the kind of honesty and follow-through that turns a nervous shopper into a buyer who trusts you. The thing you've been dreading is actually a gift, if you handle it with a little composure.

Stop fearing the question you can't answer. Start almost welcoming it. "I don't know — let me find out for you" isn't the sound of a fraud. It's the sound of a pro.

The Rule: "I don't know — let me find out for you," said calmly, builds more trust than a confident wrong answer ever will.

CHAPTER 8

STANDING TALL: PRESENCE AND COMPOSURE

CONFIDENCE SHOWS UP IN your body before it ever shows up in your words. The customer has read you before you've said hello — from how you crossed the lot, how you're standing, whether you look settled or scattered. This chapter is about that, but I want to be clear up front: this isn't a body-language lesson. Book 4 covers the mechanics. This is about one thing only — how your body either signals confidence or screams the lack of it, and how you can use it to actually become calmer.

Let me start with what insecurity looks like from the customer's side, because it's uglier than you think. The frantic salesperson. The hunched one. The one who's out of breath, talking fast, eyes darting. The customer reads all of that instantly, before a single word is processed, and it makes them uneasy. They don't think "that person seems nervous." They think "something's off here," and they put their guard up.

Here's a story that shows exactly how loud the body talks.

FROM THE FLOOR

I was sitting in the front lobby of a dealership I managed — glass front wall, full view of the lot. A car pulled in. Two salespeople inside saw it at the same time. They both jumped up, ran for the door, and literally shoved each other trying to get through it first. Pushing and shoving like it was a race.

The customers, still in their car, watched every second of this.

The one who won was out of breath when he got there. He stuck his hand out and started talking before he'd even caught his breath, never looked at the wife, never acknowledged the kids in the back seat. Just started in.

The family looked around for a few minutes and left.

When I asked what happened, the salesperson said: "They were just looking."

No. They were watching. And what they watched told them everything they needed to know about what the next hour was going to feel like. The sprint didn't just cost a deal. It answered every one of the customer's silent questions about this place — and none of the answers were good.

That family didn't leave because of anything anyone said. They left because of what the salespeople's bodies told them before anyone said anything. The shoving, the sprint, the out-of-breath pitch — that was a full conversation, and the customer heard every word of it. The salesperson thought the interaction started when he opened his mouth. It started the second they saw him through the windshield.

Now flip it. Picture the opposite salesperson. Walks out at a normal pace. Stands up straight. Unhurried. Makes eye contact, takes a breath, and says hello like he's got all the time in the world. That customer relaxes, because the body in front of them is promising calm and easy. Same lot, same car, completely different hour ahead — and not one word of difference yet.

Presence signals confidence.

So the first reason presence matters is signaling. Your posture, your pace, your breathing — these are telling the customer what the next hour is going to feel like, whether you mean them to or not. Stand tall and move slowly, and you're promising calm. Rush and fidget, and you're promising chaos. The customer believes the body over the words every tim
e.

The good news is that this is controllable. You can't always control the nervous feeling. You can absolutely control whether you walk slowly and stand straight. Even scared, you get to choose the pace of your feet.

Presence creates confidence

Here's the part most people miss, and it's the real reason I put this chapter where I did. Presence doesn't just signal confidence to the customer. It feeds confidence back to you.

This isn't a motivational line — it's how your body actually works. When you stand up straight, drop your shoulders, plant your feet, and slow your breathing down, your nervous system gets the signal that you're safe, and it starts to settle. The racing heart eases. The panicked feeling backs off a notch. You faked the calm body, and the calm body talked your nervous mind down off the ledge. Borrowed confidence becomes real, right there in your chest.

So the calm posture does double duty. It tells the customer you're confident, and it makes you more confident at the same time. That's a rare two-for-one, and it's available to you for free, on every single up.

What to actually do.

You don't need a checklist of twenty things. On the confidence angle, it comes down to three.

Slow down. Whatever pace feels natural when you're nervous, cut it in half. Walk slower. Talk slower. The rush is the tell.

Stand tall. Shoulders back, head up, weight settled. Not stiff — just upright. The hunch reads as fear; the straight back reads as ease.

Breathe. One real breath before you approach. It sounds small. It resets your whole system, and it's the fastest way to take the edge off in the moment.

That's it. Slow down, stand tall, breathe. Do those three, and you'll both look calmer and be calmer, which is the whole game.

The customer is reading your body the second they see you. Make sure it's saying something you'd want said.

The Rule: The customer reads your body before they hear your words. Slow down, stand tall, breathe — it signals calm and it makes you calm.

CHAPTER 9

HANDLING THE "No"

BACK IN CHAPTER 3, we worked on your relationship with rejection — why a "No" isn't a verdict, why it's usually not about you. That was the mindset. This chapter is the mechanics: what you actually do, in real time, in the thirty seconds after a customer tells you no. Because knowing in your head that a "No" is just information doesn't help much if your face falls and your shoulders drop the second you hear it.

Here's the situation. You've spent time with a customer. You like the deal. And they say it — not today, we're going to think about it, we're going to look around. The "No". And a new salesperson does one of a few things, all of them bad.

The three bad reactions.

The first is the flinch. Your whole body deflates. The disappointment is written all over you. The customer sees it and now feels guilty or awkward, which makes them want to leave faster. You just made your letdown their problem.

The second is the argument. You get defensive, maybe a little pushy, and you start working harder to talk them out of it. Now you've confirmed every bad thing they've ever heard about car salesmen, and a soft "No" hardens into a definite one.

The third is the collapse. You take the no, you say okay, and then you let it follow you for the next three hours. The next customer gets a deflated, defeated version of you, and they can feel it, and they walk too. One "No" became a bad afternoon.

All three come from the same place — treating the "No" like it's the end and like it's about you. We already worked on that. Now let's replace those three reactions with one good one.

Take it clean.

Taking a "No" cleanly means hearing it, accepting it without flinching, and staying exactly as warm and composed as you were thirty seconds before. No deflation. No argument. No collapse. You smile, you mean it, and you keep the door open.

Something like: "Absolutely, no pressure at all. This is a big decision, and you should be comfortable with it. Let me give you my card — and do me one favor, take my number so you've got a real person to call instead of starting over with a stranger."

Look at what that does. You honored the "No" instead of fighting it. You stayed warm, so the customer leaves thinking well of you. And you left a bridge behind. That's a confident salesperson handling a "No", not because he talked them out of it, but because he didn't fall apart when he couldn't.

The clean "No" sometimes turns.

Here's the thing nobody tells new people. How you take the "No" often decides whether it stays a no. A customer on the fence — and a lot of them are — is reading you in that exact moment. If you flinch or push, you give them a reason to be done. If you stay calm and gracious, you sometimes give them room to reconsider right there. I've watched a clean, no-pressure response turn a walking customer back around more times than I can count. Not because of a slick line. Because the calm itself was reassuring.

And even when it doesn't turn — even when they leave — the customer who left liking you is the customer who comes back, or calls, or sends their cousin. The "No" you took well is worth more than the "No" you took badly, every single time.

Protect the next up.

This is the most important part for a new salesperson, so hear me. Whatever you do, do not let this "No" touch the next customer. The next up doesn't know you just got told no. They don't care. They deserve the same fresh, calm, ready version of you that the last one got. The ability to take a "No" and walk to the next car like it never happened — that's not a personality trait. It's a discipline, and it's one of the clearest signs that a new person is going to make it.

You're going to hear "No" today, probably more than once. Take it clean. Keep your warmth. Walk to the next one whole.

The Rule: How you take the "No" decides what it costs you. Take it clean, stay warm, and never let it touch the next customer.

Chapter 10

Recovering After a Bad Interaction

A "No" is a normal part of the day. This chapter is about the other thing — the genuinely bad interaction. The customer who was rude to you for no reason. The deal you thought was done that blew up at the desk. The thing you said wrong that you're still cringing about an hour later. That's different from a no, and it hits harder.

Everybody gets these. The veteran and the rookie both. The difference isn't whether you have bad interactions — you will, all of you, regularly. The difference is what it costs you. For a seasoned salesperson, a bad one costs a few minutes. For a new one, it can cost the whole rest of the shift.

The bleed.

Here's what happens to new people, and I call it the bleed. You have a rough one — somebody's rude, or a deal falls apart, or you fumble badly — and instead of it ending when the customer leaves, it follows you. You're replaying it. You're rattled. And the next customer walks up to a salesperson who's distracted, deflated, and off his game. So that one goes badly, too. Now you've had two bad ones, which makes you more rattled, and the third feels it. One bad interaction bled into three. A bad ten minutes became a bad afternoon.

The whole skill of recovery is stopping the bleed. Containing the bad one, so it costs you that one and nothing more.

It's not about you — even when it feels like it is.

A lot of bad interactions aren't about you at all, same as we said about rejection. The rude customer was probably rude before they got out of the car. People walk onto a lot carrying a bad day, a bad marriage, a credit score they're embarrassed about, a sour experience at the last dealership. You caught the spillover. It landed on you, but it was never about you.

Now — sometimes you genuinely did mess up. You said the wrong thing, you blanked, you mishandled it. That happens too, and pretending it didn't won't help. But here's the move even then: learn the one lesson and drop the rest. Ask yourself, fast, "what would I do differently?" Get the answer. Then let go of the cringe. The lesson is useful. The replaying is not. Keep the first, dump the second.

The reset.

You need a reset — a deliberate thing you do to close out a bad interaction so it doesn't follow you. This isn't soft stuff; it's the same thing a relief pitcher does after giving up a home run. Veterans all have one, even if they've never named it.

It can be physical. Step inside, get a glass of water, walk the lot one time. A small change of scene tells your head the last thing is over.

It can be a breath and a sentence. One deep breath and a flat statement to yourself: that one's done. The next customer is brand new. Corny? Maybe. It works anyway, because you're consciously closing the file instead of letting it sit open.

It can be as simple as a reset on the walk back, so that by the time you reach the showroom door, the last one is behind you. You decide that.

Whatever it is, the point is the same. You draw a line. Bad interaction on this side. Fresh start on that side. You don't carry it across.

Give the next customer a clean slate.

The next customer had nothing to do with the last one. They didn't earn your bad mood, and they shouldn't pay for it. They deserve the same calm, ready salesperson the morning's first up got. Handing them a rattled version of you because somebody else was rude an hour ago isn't fair to them — and it's how a single bad interaction quietly wrecks your numbers for the whole day.

You will have bad ones. Plan on it. The skill isn't avoiding them. It's making sure each one costs you exactly one customer and not a single one more.

The Rule: Everybody has bad interactions. The pros just don't let them bleed. Reset, draw the line, and give the next customer a clean slate.

Chapter 11

Confidence on the Phone

Phone fear is its own animal. You might get comfortable on the lot and still freeze when you have to pick up the phone — inbound or outbound. There's a reason for that, and once you understand it, you can attack it.

Here's why the phone is scary in a way the lot isn't. On the lot you've got your whole body to work with — your smile, your posture, your presence, the car right there to point at. On the phone all of that is gone. You're a voice. And the rejection comes faster and colder: no warming up, just a quick "not interested" and a click, or a flat voice on the other end you can't read. It feels more exposed because it is more exposed.

The two kinds of phone fear.

There's the inbound call — a customer calls the store, and you're scared of saying the wrong thing, of not knowing an answer, of losing them before they ever come in. And there's the outbound call — you have to call a lead, a follow-up, somebody who didn't ask to hear from you, and the fear of bothering people, of getting shut down, can be almost paralyzing.

They feel different, but the cure is the same one that's run through this whole book: preparation, and a simple way to start.

Preparation kills phone fear too.

Remember the principle — confidence is competence you can feel. It's even more true on the phone, because on the phone, you can literally have your prep sitting in front of you. Nobody can see it.

For inbound, know your common answers cold and keep notes handy. The goal of most inbound calls isn't to sell a car over the phone — it's to set an appointment. Know that, and the call gets simpler: be warm, be helpful, answer what you can, and aim to get them in. You don't have to be perfect. You have to be pleasant and get the appointment.

For outbound, have your reason for calling and your opening line ready before you dial, with the customer's information in front of you. The fear of the cold call mostly comes from not knowing what you're going to say when they pick up — so decide before you dial. When the first ten seconds are handled, the rest is just a conversation.

A simple opening takes most of the fear out.

The scariest moment of any call is the pickup — that first second when someone's there, and now you have to talk. So script that one moment. Not the whole call, just the open. A simple, friendly, prepared first line.

For an inbound call, something steady: "Thanks for calling, this is [name], how can I help you today?" Warm, professional, done.

For an outbound follow-up: "Hi [name], this is [name] over at the dealership — you were in looking at the truck, and I told you I'd follow up, so here I am." You're not bothering them; you're doing what you said you'd do. That framing alone takes the apology out of your voice — and the apology in your voice is exactly what makes outbound calls fall flat.

When you know exactly how you're going to open, your hand stops hovering over the phone. You just pick it up and go.

Smile. They can hear it.

One small thing that sounds silly and isn't: smile when you're on the phone. People can hear it. Your voice changes. Some salespeople keep a little mirror at the desk for exactly this reason. You lost your body language on the phone, but you didn't lose your voice — and a warm voice does a lot of the work a smile would do in person.

The phone isn't a different skill. It's the same confidence, built the same way — prepare, have your opening ready, and do the reps. The first few calls are the worst. Then, like everything else in this business, it gets routine.

Pick up the phone. You already know how to do this. You just have to do it enough times to believe it.

The Rule: On the phone, you lose your body language, not your preparation. Know your opening line, smile so they can hear it, and dial.

CHAPTER 12

THE CONFIDENCE THAT COMES FROM REPS

WE'VE SPENT THIS WHOLE book building confidence from different angles — understanding the fear, preparing against it, reframing rejection, using your body, taking a "No" clean. All of it works. But I've saved the most important source of confidence for near the end, because it's the one that makes all the others permanent.

Reps.

Everything else in this book lowers the fear. Reps are what make it go away for good. The durable confidence — the kind the veterans have, the kind where nothing seems to rattle them — was not built in their heads. It was built on the floor, one customer at a time, a thousand times over.

Volume turns terrifying into routine.

Think about your very first approach. Terrifying, right? Heart pounding, mouth dry. Now think about — well, you can't yet, but trust me — your five hundredth. By then, it's nothing. You walk up to a stranger and start a conversation without a flicker of fear, the same way you'd say hello to a neighbor.

What changed between approach one and approach five hundred? Not your personality. Not some secret you learned. Just the number. You did the thing enough times that your brain finally stopped treating it like a threat. That's all confidence is, at bottom — a fear that got worn smooth by repetition.

This is why I keep coming back to reps. Because it means the thing you're most afraid of right now is temporary by definition. It cannot survive the volume. Do it enough, and it goes away. Guaranteed. The only way to lose is to not do it enough.

Chase ups. Don't avoid them.

Here's where new salespeople sabotage themselves, and I want you to see the trap clearly. The fear makes you want to avoid customers. Hang back. Let the other guy take this one. Wait for an easier-looking up. Every avoided customer feels like relief in the moment.

But every up you avoid is a rep you didn't get. You're not protecting yourself — you're starving yourself of the exact thing that would cure you. The salesperson who hides from customers stays scared, because he never piles up the volume that kills the fear. The one who chases every up he can get is scared for a few weeks and then, quietly, isn't anymore.

So flip your instinct on purpose. When part of you wants to hang back, that's the rep you most need to take. Be the one who grabs ups, not the one who ducks them. You're not just chasing today's deal. You're buying down tomorrow's fear.

What the reps build toward.

Let me show you where this goes — what a thousand approaches stacked up actually looks like.

FROM THE FLOOR

One afternoon a customer pulled into the lot in a taxi. That caught my attention — most people drive themselves in. This one stepped out and walked directly toward a specific vehicle like he already knew exactly what he was looking for.

I didn't rush. I stood up, walked out at a normal pace, gave him a small wave as I crossed the lot. When I reached him I introduced myself and told him I'd be glad to help if he had any questions.

He told me he'd just gotten off a flight and came straight from the airport. His vehicle had been destroyed in a fire in the parking lot while he was traveling. He'd seen one of our ads and came directly to us. He knew which vehicle he wanted. He just needed to drive it and confirm it.

We took a short test drive. Came back. He asked how to make out the check.

Start to finish, maybe forty-five minutes. The deal was easy because the approach was right. No pressure, no assumptions, no rushing. Just a professional greeting and a willingness to follow the customer's lead.

Not every customer comes in that ready to buy. But every customer deserves that same professional opening. You never know which one is going to be the taxi customer — the one who's already decided and just needs someone to not get in their way.

Read how I handled that. I didn't rush. I walked out at a normal pace. I didn't pounce, didn't assume, didn't oversell. I just gave a calm, professional greeting and followed his lead.

Now — could a brand-new salesperson have done that? Maybe the words. But not the calm. That unhurried ease didn't come from a technique. It came from having made that walk thousands of times, so that nothing about it spiked my heart rate anymore. The calm that closed that deal in forty-five minutes was just reps, showing up as composure.

That's what you're building toward. Not a trick. A settledness. The kind that lets you read a customer clearly and follow their lead instead of barreling through your own nerves. You can't shortcut your way to it. You can only stack the approaches until one day you notice the fear is gone and the calm is just there.

The math is on your side.

Here's the encouraging part, and it's just arithmetic. Every shift, you get more reps. Every rep, the fear gets a little smaller and the calm gets a little bigger. You don't have to do anything heroic. You just have to keep showing up and keep taking ups, and time does the rest. The veteran isn't braver than you. He's just further down the same road you're already on.

So get your reps. Take the ups nobody else wants. Be the one who goes. The fear has an expiration date, and the only thing that triggers it is volume.

Keep walking across that lot. One day soon you'll notice you forgot to be afraid.

The Rule: Confidence that lasts isn't built in your head — it's built on the floor. Chase the reps; the fear can't survive the volume.

CHAPTER 13

THE CONFIDENCE TOOLKIT

THIS LAST CHAPTER IS different. It's not an argument. It's a toolbox.

Everything in this book comes down to a handful of concrete tools, and I've put them here in one place so you can find them fast. Read this chapter before a shift to get your head right. Read it after a hard one to reset. This isn't motivation — there's no "you've got this" in here. These are tools. Use them.

Before the shift: the pre-shift routine.

Walk the lot. Know your three or four key units cold. Have your two or three opening lines ready. Get your keys, your head, and your body settled before the first car pulls in. Show up early enough that you're never scrambling. Preparation is the part of confidence you fully control — do it every shift, before the floor gets going.

When you feel the freeze: go first, go fast.

The first up is the hardest, and waiting only feeds the dread. Don't wait to feel ready — you won't. Take the first car that pulls in, before the buildup wins. The brave feeling shows up after you move, not before.

When you're afraid of rejection: it's information, not a verdict.

A "No" is almost never about you. The customer's got reasons you'll never know — a bad day, bad credit, a face that reminds them of someone.

When you hear no, don't think "I failed," think "something needs to adjust." Take the slap out of it and there's nothing left to fear.

When you don't know the answer: "Let me find out for you."

Not knowing is normal; even the veterans don't know everything. What exposes you isn't the gap — it's bluffing. Say, calmly, "Great question — I don't know off the top of my head, let me find out for you," and then go do it. It builds more trust than a confident wrong answer ever could. Fake the posture, never the facts.

When your nerves are spiking: slow down, stand tall, breathe.

Your body talks to the customer before you do — and it talks back to you. Cut your pace in half. Shoulders back, head up. Take one real breath before you approach. The calm body settles the nervous mind and tells the customer this is going to be easy. Three moves, free, every up.

When you get a "No," take it clean.

Don't flinch, don't argue, don't collapse. Stay as warm as you were a minute ago. Honor the decision, leave your card, leave a bridge back. How you take the "No" decides what it costs you — and a clean one sometimes turns.

After a bad one: reset and draw the line.

Everybody has rough interactions. The skill is not letting them bleed into the next three customers. Learn the one lesson, drop the cringe, do your reset — water, a lap of the lot, one breath and "that one's done" — and give the next customer the clean slate they deserve.

On the phone: prep beats the missing body language.

You lose your presence on a call but not your preparation, and on the phone, you can keep your prep right in front of you. Script the pickup, not the whole call. Aim inbound calls at the appointment, not the sale. Frame the outbound call as doing what you said you'd do. And smile — they can hear it.

The one that makes the rest stick: get your reps.

None of these tools work without volume. Chase ups instead of avoiding them. Every approach wears the fear a little smoother. The veteran's calm is just a thousand approaches stacked up, and you're already on the same road. Keep showing up. Keep going first. The fear has an expiration date, and reps are what trigger it.

That's the toolkit. Nothing in here is complicated. None of it asks you to be someone you're not. It just asks you to prepare, to go, and to keep going. Do that, and the confidence takes care of itself.

The Rule: Confidence isn't a feeling you wait for. It's a set of tools you use — so use them, and keep walking across the lot.

CONCLUSION

Let's go back to where we started.

I told you at the beginning that there's no confidence gene. That the fearless salesperson on your floor wasn't born that way — he just did it enough times that the fear wore off. I hope by now you believe me, because everything in this book has been pointing at that one idea: confidence is a skill, and skills are built.

You've got the tools now. You know why you freeze, and that it's normal. You know what real confidence is and that it's quiet, not loud. You know a "No" is information, not a verdict. You know preparation beats nerves, that the first up is just a tax you pay early, that "I don't know, let me find out" is a strength, that your body can talk your nerves down, that a bad one doesn't have to bleed, and that the phone is the same skill with the lights off. And you know the one that ties it all together: reps.

Here's what I want you to do with all of it. Not much, actually. Just go to work tomorrow and use one thing. Take the first up fast. Or take a "No" clean. Or walk out slow and stand tall. Pick one and do it. Then do it again the next day. That's the whole method. Confidence is built one shift at a time, the same way it's built for everyone who's ever made it in this business.

You're going to be scared tomorrow. Probably the next day too. That's fine. Being scared and going anyway is the entire job at the start — and every time you go anyway, the fear gets a little smaller. You don't have to wait until you're not afraid. You just have to walk across the lot while you still are.

Nobody handed me confidence. I built it, slow, on hot lots and slow days, one customer at a time, and so will you. You're closer than you think. The only thing standing between you and the calm version of yourself is a pile of approaches you haven't made yet.

So go make them.

I'll see you on the floor.

Tips for the Sales Manager

A word to the managers, since you're the ones who decide how fast these new people get good — or whether they make it at all.

Everything in this book is aimed at the new salesperson. But you have more influence over their confidence than the book ever will. A new hire spends a few hours with these pages and forty hours a week with you. What you do on the floor matters more than anything I can write.

So here's what I learned managing new people for a lot of years.

Their problem is rarely knowledge. It's nerve.

You'll be tempted to fix a struggling new salesperson with more product training. Usually, that's not it. Most of them know more than they're showing — they just can't make themselves get out there and use it. Before you pile on more to learn, ask whether the real problem is fear. If it is, coaching them on tow ratings won't help. Getting them across the lot will.

Make it safe to be new.

A terrified new salesperson is a salesperson who'll bluff, hide, and avoid ups — all the things that get them washed out. The fastest way to fix that is to take the terror down. Let them know mistakes are expected and survivable. The new person who isn't scared of you is far more willing to take the scary up. Fear of the boss stacks right on top of fear of the customer, and you can remove one of those for free.

Push them toward reps, gently.

You read Chapter 12 — confidence comes from volume. Your job is to keep them in the volume. Don't let a nervous new hire quietly hide at the back of the lot taking one up a day. Get them out there. Not by barking at them, but by making the next approach feel small and routine. "Go grab that one, just say hello, I've got your back." Every up you nudge them into is a rep that buys down their fear.

Coach the moment, not the month.

A two-minute debrief right after an interaction is worth more than an hour of classroom training. While it's fresh: what went well, one thing to try next time, done. Keep it short and specific. New people can't absorb ten corrections — they can absorb one. Give them the one.

Catch them being good.

New salespeople measure themselves only by cars sold, and early on, that number is brutal. If selling units is the only thing you recognize, you'll lose people who were two weeks from breaking through. Notice the other things — a smooth greeting, a clean recovery after a rough customer, the fact that they took every up today instead of hiding. Those are the leading indicators. Name them out loud. It's how you keep a good person in the seat long enough to get good.

Be the calm on the floor.

Your people read you the way customers read them. If you're frantic, short-tempered, and visibly stressed when it's slow, they catch it. If you're steady, they catch that instead. The calm veteran salesperson usually came up under a calm manager. Be the presence you want them to develop.

Confident salespeople create better customer experiences, and confident salespeople are mostly made — by managers who made it safe to learn, kept them in the reps, and noticed when they got something right. That's the job. Do it well, and you won't just hit this month's number. You'll build people who hit numbers for years.

Appendix

The Rules

Every chapter in this book ends with a single rule — the one principle from that chapter built to stick. Here they are in one place. Read them before a shift to get your head right, or after a hard one to remember what the job actually asks of you.

Introduction

Confidence is not something you're born with. It's something you build — so start building.

Chapter 1

The customer can't tell the difference between your fear and not caring. From across the lot, both look like nobody came to help.

Chapter 2

Real confidence is quiet. If you have to perform it, it isn't confidence — it's insecurity in a louder shirt.

Chapter 3

A "No" is information, not a verdict. And most of the time, it isn't even about you.

Chapter 4

You can't talk yourself out of fear. But you can prepare your way out of it.

Chapter 5

The first up is the hardest one you'll make all day. So make it fast — before the dread has time to grow.

Chapter 6

Fake the posture, never the facts. Acting calm builds confidence; bluffing a customer destroys trust the second you're caught.

Chapter 7

"I don't know — let me find out for you," said calmly, builds more trust than a confident wrong answer ever will.

Chapter 8

The customer reads your body before they hear your words. Slow down, stand tall, breathe — it signals calm, and it makes you calm.

Chapter 9

How you take the "No" decides what it costs you. Take it clean, stay warm, and never let it touch the next customer.

Chapter 10

Everybody has bad interactions. The pros just don't let them bleed. Reset, draw the line, and give the next customer a clean slate.

Chapter 11

On the phone, you lose your body language, not your preparation. Know your opening line, smile so they can hear it, and dial.

Chapter 12

Confidence that lasts isn't built in your head — it's built on the floor. Chase the reps; the fear can't survive the volume.

Chapter 13

Confidence isn't a feeling you wait for. It's a set of tools you use — so use them, and keep walking across the lot.

ALSO AVAILABLE

What Drives Customers Away in the First Minute

Book 10 — The First Five Minutes With a Car Buyer

How to Transition from Greeting to Conversation and Move Toward the Sale

WORK WITH BRUCE

If you're interested in one-on-one coaching, sales team training, or dealership consulting, Bruce works with individuals and organizations through Life Guidance Consulting.

For inquiries:

www.lifeguidanceconsulting.com

bruce@lifeguidanceconsulting.com

For publishing inquiries or bulk orders:

www.bedrockheritagepublishing.com

info@bedrockheritagepublishing.com

About the Author

Bruce Huddleston spent thirty-five years in the automotive industry, working every level of the business from showroom floor salesperson to finance manager, sales manager, used car manager, and general manager. His career included new-car franchise dealerships, independent used-car operations, and a decade in buy-here, pay-here — giving him a breadth of experience that few in the industry can match.

He began as a high school dropout who needed a job and ended up discovering a profession. He ended as a veteran who had trained hundreds of salespeople, managed multiple departments, and built a reputation for straight talk in an industry that doesn't always reward it.

Since retiring, Bruce has opened a life coaching practice, assists his wife with her mental health therapy practice, and operates Bedrock Heritage Publishing, a division of Life Guidance Consulting LLC, where he writes practical guides for sales professionals across multiple industries.

The Complete Car Sales Survival Guide is his flagship work. The Car Sales Survival Guide Series — a collection of focused training guides on specific sales skills — is built on the same foundation of real experience, honest insight, and zero tolerance for the kind of nonsense that gives sales a bad name.

He lives in Tyler, Texas.

A Quick Favor

If Car Sales Confidence for New Salespeople helped you — if it changed how you walk onto a lot, how you read a customer, or how you think about what your body is saying before you open your mouth — I'd be grateful if you'd take two minutes to leave a review wherever you bought it.

Reviews matter more than most people realize. They help other salespeople find books that can actually make a difference in their work. And honest feedback helps me keep writing things worth reading.

You can simply scan the QR code below.

https://www.amazon.com/review/create-review/?asin=1972179160

www.bedrockheritagepublishing.com

Thank you for spending time with this book. Now go to work.

— Bruce Huddleston

www.ingramcontent.com/pod-product-compliance
Lightning Source LLC
Chambersburg PA
CBHW061312140726
47998CB00006B/2360